More Book Please
A Baby Sign Language Book
Copyright © 2021 by Nancy Lynch

Sign Language / Language

ISBN-13:	Paperback:	978-1-64749-306-6
	Hardback:	978-1-64749-307-3
	ePub:	978-1-64749-308-0

All rights reserved. No part of this publication may be reproduced, distributed, or transmitted in any form or by any means, including photocopying, recording, or other electronic or mechanical methods, without the prior written permission of the publisher or author, except in the case of brief quotations embodied in critical reviews and certain other noncommercial uses permitted by copyright law.

Although every precaution has been taken to verify the accuracy of the information contained herein, the author and publisher assume no responsibility for any errors or omissions. No liability is assumed for damages that may result from the use of information contained within.

Printed in the United States of America

GoTo Publish

GoToPublish LLC
1-888-337-1724
www.gotopublish.com
info@gotopublish.com

Table of Contents

More..4

All Done...10

Eat..14

Drink..16

Please..18

Thank You...20

Steps to Baby Sign Success..24

More Book Please
A Baby Sign Language Book

Nancy Lynch

I am a big kid
And growing up every day,
Listen to my story,
And what I must say.

I can Jump, and I can walk,
Now it's time for me to talk.

The words are Locked inside my head,
They want to come out, and be said.

I know lots of things I want to say,
Such as "I love you Mom", and "Let's go play".

It's time to learn how to baby sign,
Sign what I want, and what is mine.

I Love you

When we are playing on the floor,
I don't want it to end, I want more.

More, more, more is a sign that is fun,
Another new sign, is I am all done.

All done, all done, something needs to stop,
Such as if I eat too much, and am ready to pop.

But if I am hungry from my head to my feet,
It is dinner or snack time, so let's eat, eat, eat.

When I am thirsty and go to the sink,
Juice, milk, or water is what I want to drink.

The sign for drink looks right, I think,
From a bottle or cup, I drink, drink, drink.

Mommy says there is a word I should know,
A polite word to say,
And show how much I grow.

Please is a word, to say at the end.
It fixes the wrongs, and makes them mend.
So when something is very important to me,

I simply say and sign please, please, please.

Another polite word that you should learn,
It is a good one to practice when it is your turn.

When someone gives you a balloon that is blue,
The response that you say, is a simple thank you.

Thank you, thank you is a magical phrase,
Say it often and you will get big praise.

Now the words are not trapped in my head,
Baby sign shows you what i want instead.

It is now time for this book to end,
Now go and share it with your favorite friend.

Steps to Baby Sign Success

1. Start Small: Unless you are familiar with sign language it can be overwhelming, so pick 3-5 signs to start with.
2. Start with Basic Signs: Success is with familiar words.
3. Repeat, Repeat, Repeat: Repetition is the key!
4. Always Pair Sign with Word: Speaking is the goal, so always pair the sign with the word. If your baby signs to you, acknowledge the request by saying the word.
5. Be Patient! Signing is learning a new language, some babies pick it up faster than others. Don't give up and keep your baby's age in mind.
6. Allow for Flexibility: You can make up your own sign or modify an existing one, BUT be consistent when using it.